RSPB

RSPB

first book of
trees

Derek Niemann

A & C BLACK
AN IMPRINT OF BLOOMSBURY
LONDON   NEW DELHI   NEW YORK   SYDNEY

Published 2012 by A&C Black,
An imprint of Bloomsbury Publishing Plc
50 Bedford Square, London WC1B 3DP
www.bloomsbury.com

ISBN: 978-1-4081-6570-6

Printed in China by C & C Offset Printing Co., Ltd.

A&C Black uses paper produced from elemental
chlorine-free pulp, harvested from managed
sustainable forests.

10 9 8 7 6 5 4 3 2

MIX
Paper from
responsible sources
FSC® C008047
FSC
www.fsc.org

Contents

Trees

Trees grow in all shapes and sizes. Some are taller than houses. Some are little bushes. Some are skinny. Others have really thick trunks!

This book will help you name many of the trees you will see in towns, cities and the countryside. Find out about their flowers and their fruit. Learn about the shapes of their leaves. Which tree gives us hazelnuts? And does a hornbeam tree really have horns?

At the back of this book is a Spotter's Guide to help you remember the trees you find. You could also draw them in summer and winter. Why not collect the fallen leaves?

Turn the page to find out more about trees!

Silver birch

This tree is named for its silvery-white trunk. It grows very fast. A silver birch will be as tall as you when it is only three years old.

Birch twigs were once used to make brooms.

Thin branches

Flaky, silver bark

Catkins in April

Black poplar

All poplar trees have broad leaves with very pointy tips. There are male poplar trees and female poplar trees. If there are no male trees nearby, then the females can not make any seeds.

Green female catkins. Male catkins are red.

Fluffy seeds appear in early summer

Poplar wood is used to make matches.

Aspen

The leaves of this tree flutter in the breeze. If you get close, it sounds like they are whispering.

Female catkins drop fluffy seeds in May

Rounded leaves with jagged edges

Lime

The leaves of this tree look like little hearts. Limes flower in July. Bees love drinking their nectar.

The limes we eat don't come from these lime trees!

A lime tree in winter

Heart-shaped leaves

Guelder rose

The guelder rose has pretty leaves, flowers and berries. In the wild, it usually grows in damp parts of a wood. People plant this tree in their gardens.

Bright red, shiny berries

White flowers in May and June

Middle part of the leaf sticks out

Blackthorn

This is a very prickly bush – watch out! Look for it growing in hedges. The fruits are called sloes. They taste very sour.

Long, sharp thorns

White flowers in early spring

Small leaves

Round, blue-black berries, often covered in white dust

Holly

These prickly trees have red berries. You will often see them at Christmas on cards or decorations. Holly leaves stay on the tree all year round.

The spines on the leaves point in different directions. This might be to stop the animals eating them.

Spines

Berries in late autumn

Sessile oak

The word sessile means without a stalk. The acorns on these trees grow straight out of the twig. Acorns on common oak trees grow on stalks.

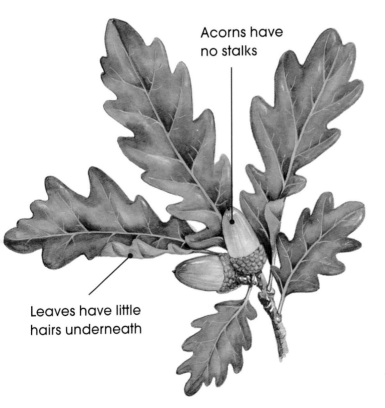

Acorns have no stalks

Leaves have little hairs underneath

Sallow

Another name for this small tree is pussy willow. If you stroke the grey catkins, they feel as soft as a cat's fur. Goldfinches use the fluffy seeds to give their nests a soft lining.

Pussy willow catkins appear in January before the leaves. They turn yellow in March.

Furry white female flowers (catkins)

Short, pointed leaves with tiny teeth

Hairy underneath

Alder

Look for alder trees next to streams and rivers. They don't mind having their roots under water! You can spot this tree in winter by its little cones.

Dark brown bark

Little cones often stay on the tree until the spring

Leaves are almost round

Catkins

Hazel

Pigeons, jays, squirrels and mice all want to eat the fruit of the hazel tree. And so do we! The hazelnuts on this tree are the same as the ones you can buy in shops.

Often grows as a bush rather than a tree

Nuts ripen in their shells in early autumn

Leaves have zig-zag edges

16

Hornbeam

The name hornbeam comes from two words meaning hard tree. Its wood is very strong. In autumn, its leaves turn orange and yellow.

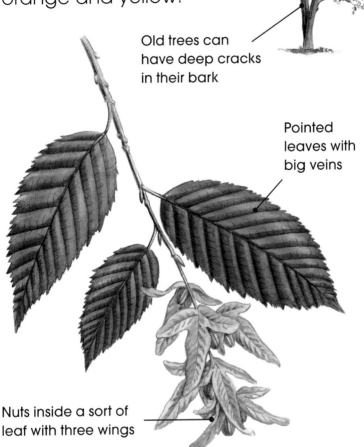

Old trees can have deep cracks in their bark

Pointed leaves with big veins

Nuts inside a sort of leaf with three wings

Beech

You will often find lots of these trees growing together. They have tall trunks and the leaves and branches grow from a long way up.

Wood mice feed on beech nuts in the winter.

Small triangular nuts drop from spiny cases in autumn

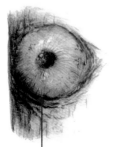

Round mark where a branch fell off a long time ago

Wavy-edged, smooth leaves

English elm

This tree does not grow much bigger than a bush. Before it dies, it sends out underground suckers. New elm trees sprout from the suckers to take its place.

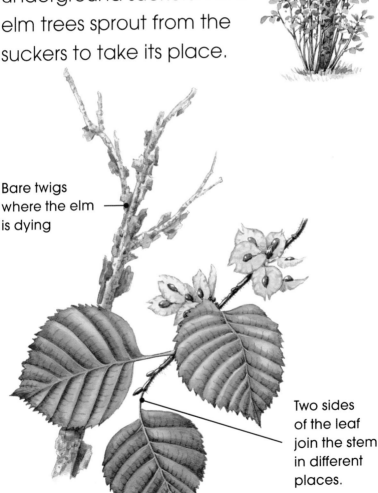

Bare twigs where the elm is dying

Two sides of the leaf join the stem in different places.

19

Crab apple

This is the oldest apple tree.
We can eat the apples,
but they are small,
hard and bitter.

White blossom
in spring

Sharp thorns
on twigs

Apples turn red or
yellow as they ripen

Wayfaring tree

You will usually find these little trees in hedges and at the edges of woods. Look for their white flowers in spring.

Dozens of little flowers close together.

Red berries turn black as they ripen

The berries on this tree taste horrible to us but birds eat them.

Pairs of leaves grow opposite each other

Walnut

The crinkly nuts that we buy from shops come from the walnut tree. This tree was brought to this country a long time ago and now some grow in the wild.

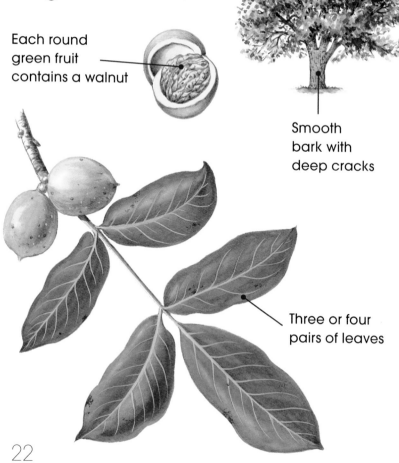

Each round green fruit contains a walnut

Smooth bark with deep cracks

Three or four pairs of leaves

Cherry

Look for white cherry blossom in spring. Wild cherry trees flower in April. Bird cherry trees flower in May.

Cherry bark splits into thick bands around the tree

White flowers come out before the leaves

Leaf stems are red

Wild cherry berries are red. Bird cherry berries are black

Sweet chestnut

The Romans brought the sweet chestnut to Britain. But they did not realise it would be too cold here for this tree. That is why our chestnuts do not grow very big.

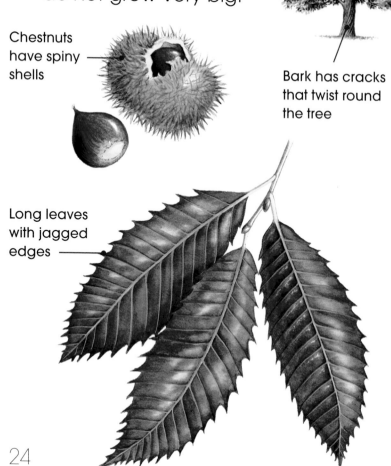

Chestnuts have spiny shells

Bark has cracks that twist round the tree

Long leaves with jagged edges

24

Willow

Willow trees have long, thin leaves and live in wet places. When they are old, their trunks often crack open.

Grey bark

Female catkins turn into white flowers in July

Long, yellow male catkins in early spring

Willow branches are often cut at the top of the trunk. It makes the trees live longer. New branches will grow back.

Sycamore

This huge tree can be wider than it is tall. It produces lots of giant leaves and seeds. Sycamores were brought here from other countries.

Seeds have little wings to help them fly away

Smooth grey bark turns brown and cracks as the tree gets older

Leaves bigger than your hand

Field maple

Look for the gold and yellow leaves of field maple in woods in autumn. All of the trees in the maple family have lovely autumn colours.

Small, round-headed tree

Leaves have rounded edges. They change colour from green to gold before they fall

Two seeds are stuck together

London plane

This tall tree is found in London's streets and squares, and in other towns and cities too. Look for the patchy bark on the trunk.

Bark with yellow and brown patches

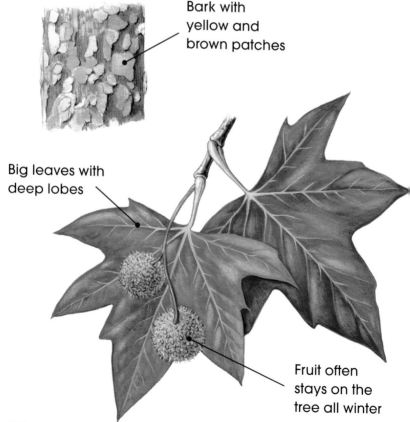

Big leaves with deep lobes

Fruit often stays on the tree all winter

Hawthorn

Prickly hedges in the countryside are often made of hawthorn bushes. Hawthorn can also grow into a tree. They have white or pink flowers and red berries.

Rough bark with lots of cracks

Small leaves

Lots of white flowers in spring

Red berries in autumn

Hawthorn is sometimes called the May tree because its white flowers come out in that month.

Sharp thorns

Common oak

Oak trees grow from little acorns into some of the biggest trees in the wood. They can have very thick trunks and live for hundreds of years.

Leaves with wavy edges

Acorns on long stalks

Horse chestnut

This is a very big tree. In spring, it has big flowers that stick up like white candles. In autumn, it has shiny nuts called conkers.

Prickly conker cases

White or pink flowers

Shiny conkers

Big leaves like giant's fingers

Children play a game called conkers with chestnuts.

Ash

Ash is a very tall tree. In winter, look out for the black buds on the tips of its twigs.

Black buds

Long, slim leaves come out in May

Seeds are called keys and hang in little bunches. Each seed has a little wing

Rowan

This tree is also called mountain ash. It grows higher up the hills than most other trees. People plant it in their gardens too.

Smooth bark

Rowans used to be planted in gardens and churchyards to scare away witches!

Bright red berries in autumn

Small leaves with little pointed teeth

Elder

You will find elder in all sorts of places. Birds eat the berries and spread the seeds in their droppings. Most elders only grow as big as a bush.

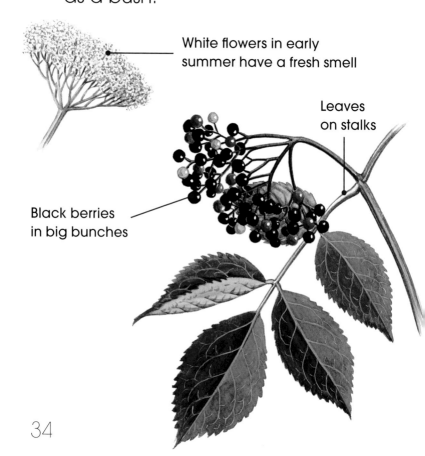

White flowers in early summer have a fresh smell

Leaves on stalks

Black berries in big bunches

Larch

The larch has leaves that look like needles, just like other trees called conifers. But the larch is the only conifer that drops all of its leaves in winter.

Leaves turn gold in autumn before they fall.

A larch in winter

Pink female flowers

Yellow male flowers

Cone

Spruce

Your Christmas tree is probably a spruce. Spruce trees originally grew in northern countries. Now they are also grown here in big woods.

Leaves like needles. They stay on the tree all year round

Long brown cone with scales

Little male flowers are yellow and red

Scots pine

These trees can live for a long time – about 250 years. As they grow old, their trunks get much thicker. The very old trees are known as granny pines.

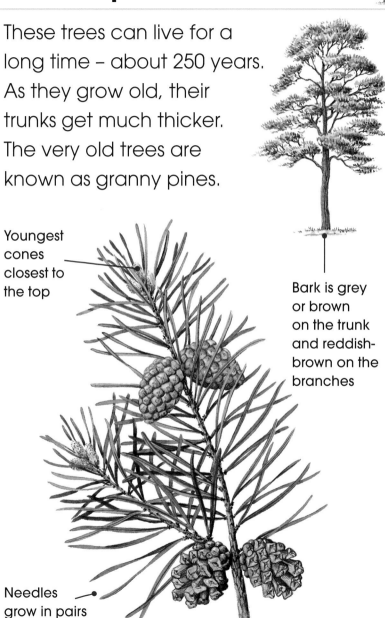

Youngest cones closest to the top

Bark is grey or brown on the trunk and reddish-brown on the branches

Needles grow in pairs

Leyland cypress

Leyland cypress trees are often grown as garden hedges. Sometimes they do turn into proper trees. They can grow taller than you in one year!

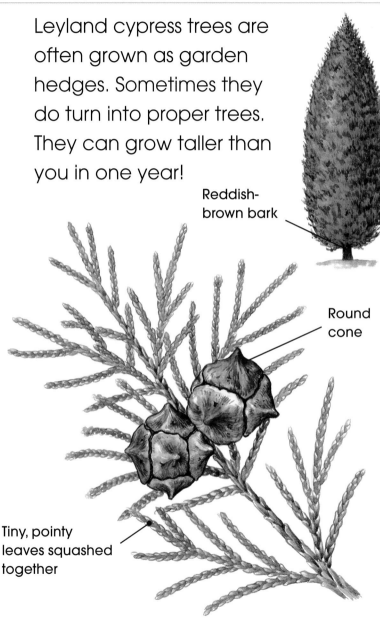

Reddish-brown bark

Round cone

Tiny, pointy leaves squashed together

Cedar

This giant tree often grows in parks or in big gardens. It keeps its needles through the winter.

Dark green needles

Huge branches

Seeds drop out one by one when the cone is ripe. They leave a bare stalk on the tree.

Hard cones with seeds packed tightly inside

Look for seeds scattered on the ground.

Yew

The yew can live longer than any other tree in Britain. Some yew trees are over a thousand years old. It has pretty berries but they are very poisonous to us.

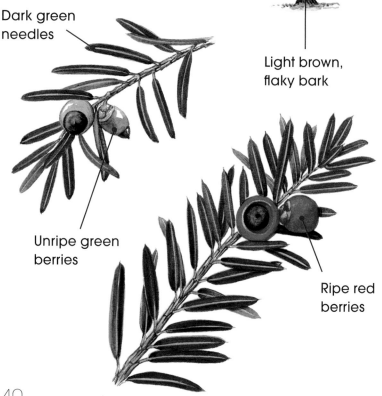

Dark green needles

Light brown, flaky bark

Unripe green berries

Ripe red berries

Useful words

blossom a tree's flowers

bud small growth on a plant that turns into a leaf, flower or shoot

conifer evergreen tree that keeps its leaves in the winter

nectar the sweet liquid that flowers make to attract insects

needles sharp, pointed leaves of evergreen trees

nut fruit with a hard shell

pollen tiny grains that are made in the male parts of a flower

sapling young, skinny tree

Spotter's guide

How many of these trees have you seen? Tick them when you spot them.

Silver birch
page 6

Black poplar
page 7

Aspen
page 8

Lime
page 9

Guelder rose
page 10

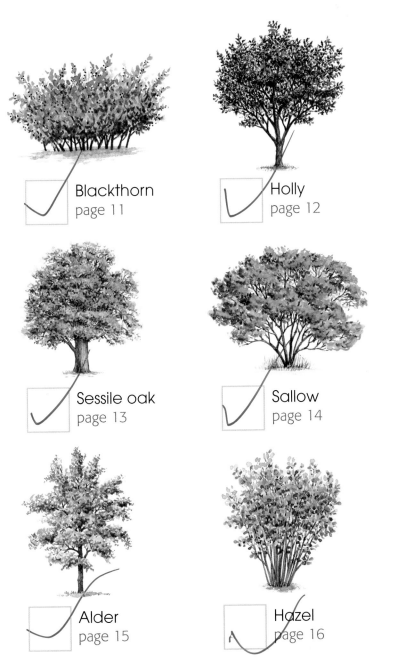

☐ Blackthorn
page 11

☐ Holly
page 12

☐ Sessile oak
page 13

☐ Sallow
page 14

☐ Alder
page 15

☐ Hazel
page 16

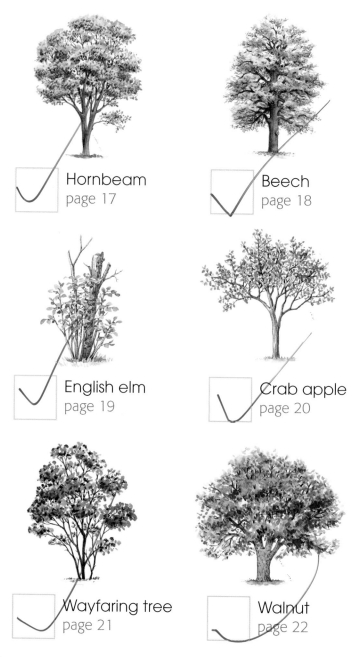

Hornbeam
page 17

Beech
page 18

English elm
page 19

Crab apple
page 20

Wayfaring tree
page 21

Walnut
page 22

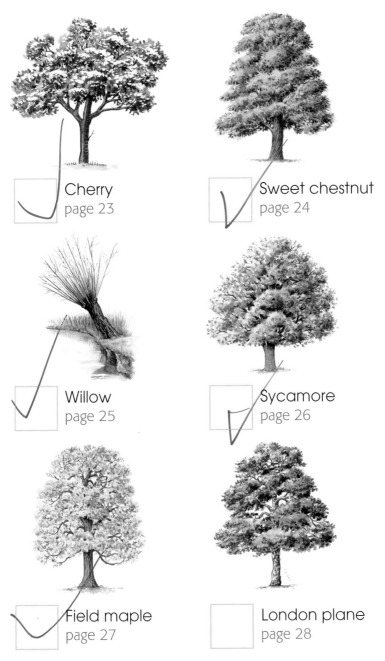

Cherry
page 23

Sweet chestnut
page 24

Willow
page 25

Sycamore
page 26

Field maple
page 27

London plane
page 28

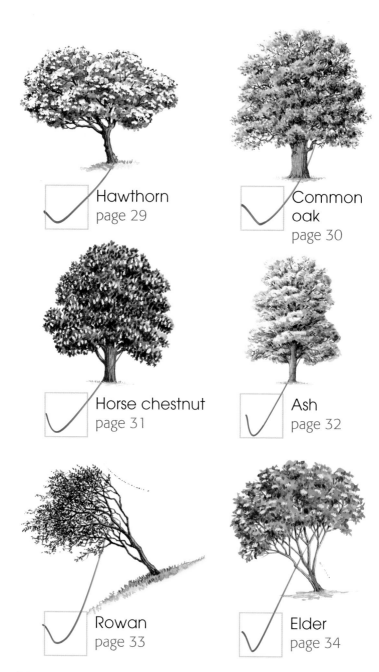

Hawthorn
page 29

Common oak
page 30

Horse chestnut
page 31

Ash
page 32

Rowan
page 33

Elder
page 34

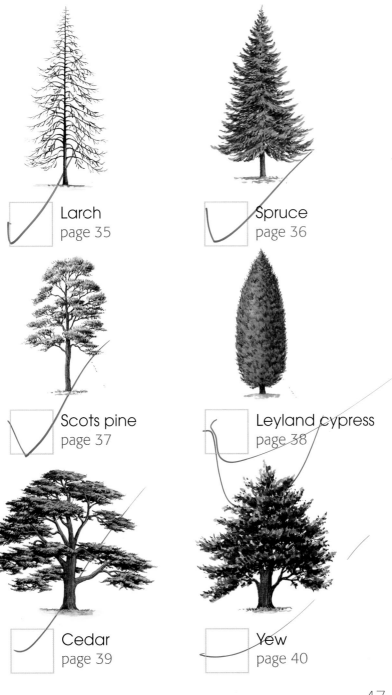

Larch
page 35

Spruce
page 36

Scots pine
page 37

Leyland cypress
page 38

Cedar
page 39

Yew
page 40

Find out more

If you have enjoyed this book you might like our club for children. RSPB Wildlife Explorers helps you learn more about nature. You will get a magazine six times a year that tells you all about things you can do.

Visit the world's biggest wildlife club for children at www.rspb.org.uk/youth